TOTAL PARTY KILL

TOTAL PARTY KILL

POEMS

CRAIG FRANCIS POWER

BREAKWATER
P.O. Box 2188, St. John's, NL, Canada, A1C 6E6
WWW.BREAKWATERBOOKS.COM

LIBRARY AND ARCHIVES CANADA CATALOGUING IN PUBLICATION
Title: Total party kill / Craig Francis Power.
Names: Power, Craig Francis, 1974- author.
Identifiers: Canadiana 20240375416 | ISBN 9781778530296 (softcover)
Subjects: LCGFT: Poetry.
Classification: LCC PS8631.O839 T68 2024 | DDC C811/.6—dc23

We acknowledge the support of the Canada Council for the Arts. We acknowledge the financial support of the Government of Canada and the Government of Newfoundland and Labrador through the Department of Tourism, Culture, Industry and Innovation for our publishing activities.

Printed and bound in India by Imprint Press.

Canada Council for the Arts | Conseil des Arts du Canada | Canada | Newfoundland Labrador

Breakwater Books is committed to choosing papers and materials for our books that help to protect our environment. To this end, this book is printed on a recycled paper that is certified by the Forest Stewardship Council®.

THIS BOOK IS DEDICATED TO
THE MEMORY OF GIUSEPPE POP,
WHO DIED AMONGST FRIENDS.

CONTENTS

THE BEASTLANDS

THE NINE HELLS

LIMBO

THE ABYSS

THE PRIME MATERIAL PLANE

THE BEASTLANDS

TOMB OF ANNIHILATION

We dip silk ropes tied at their ends with hooded lanterns into the maw under an excavated tile and plunge the narrow beams of light into the underneath where very little has moved in centuries, or so we're told, but I trust no one—particularly you, my friend, whose dice rolls would be pure magic if we didn't know you're fudging them so you can win. You can't—things just go on until they don't.

But at my first meeting, after I hit bottom finally and crawled to the church and down into its basement crypt that smelled of instant coffee, the Coffee-mate and sugar cubes yellow with fly vomit, the rectangles of poisonous light, there was a clutch of congregated ghouls—revenants they're also called—chewing ligaments and spearmint gum so old it's tar holding up the brickwork. They saved my life. Today, at least.

I drop down first, seeing through the dark. It's my role in this party—drinking myself to death. Grasping vines, the undergrowth, the broken earth: difficult terrain. The trauma of generations distilled into my character, a sheet of paper. Beneath my boots that make no sound, the stones are slick with dew, the air as thick as the hair your dad still had before he died bitter in his hospital bed, and dreamed of home, its jungles and its steam.

THE FORGE OF FURY

Secret among us there lives a race of wraiths who drain the bodies of the townsfolk dry out where the white woods have been burned to ash as firebreak. They hang the skins like plastic bags or Old Man's Beard from the limbs of trees and then take their victim's place, sleep in their beds and work the fields, at sea or forge—for they think being poor is cool, as Jarvis Cocker once observed—and have beset our wells with incantations old as castes, with spider webs and gristle, with wyvern spurs, belladonna, monkshood, all the nightshade in the world. It fucks us up and blinds us, dreaming where we stand.

There is no getting out—the songs they sing are ours. Likewise the hands with which they grasp the wooden handles of our tools that in truth were never really ours, for they serve our liege, whose bannermen, our Lords, hold flags and pennants in the wind burning brightly with the fruit of all our blood and rage—to which we still yet genuflect.

SCOURGE OF THE SLAVE LORDS

After four years of freedom from captivity our friend returned to bend his head beneath the whip, spent a week in a hotel room where he could not be found by anyone, especially himself. Let his eyes unfocus so that revealed in the pattern of the carpet was the face of Gruumsh, the One-Eyed God of Orcs. Whose rage is legendary. Whose resentment is legendary. Whose lust is legendary. Whose rage is scavenged scraps of armour, strips of leather, and an ax and a club and the hand that wields the club. His rage is the hand that wields the whip, is the same as that of our friend dialling room service, the same as that which brings a mouth as cold as iron to his lips to drink. It is the same as that of Gruumsh, the One-Eyed God of Orcs. Was it the pandemic, the bankruptcy, the divorce, the brain tumour, the spasms that resulted from the tumour? Or was it none of these?

Why should it be that the world spins around the sun? The moon around the earth? Why should it be that there is such a thing as winter and such a thing as night with stars as sharp and as precise as the point of light in the eye of this one and terrible god to whom we all must bow our heads?

THE LOST MINE OF PHANDELVER

The sex we have is too hot to be true, but it is. My sponsor warned against replacing one drug with another. The gleaming mithral tracks beneath the ground run toward a molten core where, the townsfolk say, there was a portal from whence the demon lords once crawled, born out of ooze as slick as the high-end lube we use for anal.

Orcus, Demon Prince of the Undead, sweeps his skull-tipped wand before her eyes. Enthralled she swears an oath of her devotion. She whispers her devotion. Her devotion is an ecstasy. The tusks in his piggy face point up, like me, pearled with dew my girlfriend drinks with gusto, and with glee.

SLEEPING DRAGON'S WAKE

My next-to-last panic attack hit flush—without warning—when I beheld the death knight's dreadnought beached upon the shore, near where the faithful built their shrine to Talos, god of storms, whose hangovers are only slightly less prodigious than his cruel and playful rage.

For indeed it was a wave. A swell conceived at the bottom of the ocean floor. A tectonic pulse when my mom described a small and simple fable from my father's childhood, but I don't remember much. A belt. A public whipping. The kids lined up against a fence for the crime of speech.

Three months without a drink, and I'm told the newly sober are prone to such afflictions. Prone to knock-off Valium that isn't habit-forming, though I'm agnostic to that claim. In the fine-dining place I worked before I quit, I'd serve this very doctor endless shots of vodka and chartreuse, which is merely further proof that money doesn't buy you taste. Plus, his tips were shit.

But in the undertow I wondered, does the dragon sleep so peacefully because it's certain to one day come awake? Beneath its lidded eyes does it see the smouldered bodies of the townsfolk strewn across the fields? Does it fear its stint to come in federal prison? Does it dream and wish to slip into the past like a wisp of smoke and swoop above this town to unleash its fiery breath?

DRAGONS OF DESPAIR

for Steve C.

Now that he can say that there is no escape, the gods at last return to the land of Krynn. Who can blame a bard, a thief, a fighter, or a mage for being who they are when the clerics are bereft of vision, and teach us, through their example, only what's best not to do?

The daughter that he left behind? The manic pixie dream girl that he matched on Tinder? Whom he says he's sure he would have one day married, had things gone the other way. The seagull with a crust of pizza in its beak? The metal edges of the dumpster's mouth, gleaming in the light cast down by his god's one bright and burning eye, here, here, before our meeting, in the church's parking lot?

THE TEMPLE OF ELEMENTAL EVIL

In the aftermath of the Battle of Emridy Meadows, where at last the horde of evil humanoids was broken, what else is there to do about the floor once you've paced a thousand miles into its laminate, rearranged the furniture so many times you've scratched a madman's portrait into its face, and most likely forsaken your deposit, but grab the mop, take down the vinegar and bleach, fill the bucket with steaming water, and set about to make it gleam as best you can?

For, after three hundred and some odd days of this, there was no flash of light, no parting of the clouds, no god, no angel floating down like I'd been promised, and I was bored, bored, bored, bored, bored as the man who's killed the monster and bedded the king's most treasured daughter. Ignoring my sponsor's calls, without the friendly anguish even of a morning after.

Could it be as common as wanting to get laid? Wanting to be liked? Wanting to be cool? Could it be as simple as feeling less alone? Or more alone? To set the tongues to wag, the petticoats to rustle? Could it be as plain as the mounted heads, the VLTs, the classic rock, the two-dollar shots at the hotel bar in which I find myself, so casually and utterly and suddenly insane?

AGAINST THE CULT OF THE REPTILE GOD

Forced to leave the only home I've known, from the deck I saw my mother and my daughter down there waving from the docks, where their scarves blew straight out from the wind and the shadows of the birds whirled across the trembling boards. Far to the south of here our friend was taken captive. We got his text saying to send help and determined by rolling dice which of the citizens would go. In the public square I rolled a one and squeezed my daughter's hand. I don't want her to know what the townsfolk always say—that we were born unlucky—but I believe it to be true.

The masts bedecked with streaming flags, the sea was rough with chop and spray, we saw the merfolk dive beneath the waves. They led us to a town perched atop a range of ferrous cliffs stained red, its beacon webbed in fog. We heard its bell and in my dreams beneath the deck I heard a chime, the vibration of my phone, and woke and thought of him, how my daughter loved him, called him uncle, ran behind his horse and cried as he rode out of town and weeping fell down to the ground, dust from the hooves in clouds around her.

CASTLE AMBER (CHÂTEAU D' AMBERVILLE)

for G.G.

The whole thing puts me in mind of a mosquito trapped in tree sap. A house sprung up from the ground like a holly bush wherein yellow jewels hop branch to branch, scarlet berries in their beaks.

At the San Diego Comic Con this paunchy tie-dyed cokehead geezer is a god, sucked off by starlets hoping for a role in what, exactly? This god who only ever meant to make a buck, fiddling in his basement, stealing from his friends—ideas or wives or money—and who am I to judge?

Primary amongst the monsters here this thin prince transformed into a wolf—how could a castle such as this, facing south and east, be so bereft of sunlight?

My first fifth step my sponsor said the point was to understand the nature of your wrongs. Not the acts themselves but rather what their essence was.

A treasure within this earthen vessel was how he learned the works of God move through the world within us all, passing one into the other.

DEAD GODS

In the dream I've had a thousand times since before the cataclysm, trained with weapons forged not in the fire but beneath the slip-rope in this living room on Fleming Street, from an online boxing course I bought six months ago with money earned from waiting tables, it's not the man as he is now, the spindly retired dredge operator, whose face I batter to a pulp—with hooks and uppercuts set up by slips and steps and feints and jabs and straights—but the one from forty years ago, back when I was young enough to believe in make-believe, that digging in the earth could change the course of anything.

THE NINE HELLS

INFERNAL MACHINE REBUILD

Atop this cliff that overlooks the glowing sea these kings and queens destroyed when the demons they had summoned dragged the floor for gold and killed the fish-folk fleets who'd served as serfs for years, that great unwashed who broke themselves on rocks where waves of jade and foam struck ground and glowed in loam and kelp as dark and dead as the eyes of tomcod, I've been invited to a party amongst the merely talentless and beautiful, the dull and filthy rich.

The castle and its grounds fragrant with currants bunched from their slender veins. The slurry brimming country-china bowls with gore that feeds their elegance, pearls their eyes and hearts with sepia. Centuries of wealth, clotted cream and scones and clots and tea and tapioca. Silver knives in sunlight, a glass of sherry, the lit tip of a cigar—its plume describes a galleon misting sky with cannon-smoke and flak, its hold filled with bones and souls that plum the sea with blood.

Dad stalked this very land for ducks and partridge, back before our dog went mad and led him pointless through the woods, would shoot its nose into an empty bush, a sky. A rifle-bolt flicked over, and a bolt of fear shot through me. A Blue Belton at his boots put down out back behind our house when the fever took its mind and it frothing rolled in sodden bog and mud. Near here the Catholics ripped their church to rubble—either lost their faith or died or both, thank God, and sold the lot for legal costs. The shadow that its mountain makes bleeds along the ground.

THE LOST CAVERNS OF TSOJCANTH

for Mark Callanan

By now almost everyone has heard the news, but should you find yourself counted amongst the benighted few who haven't, this paladin would be pleased to bless you with the gift of fire, how he slept for seven hundred years on an alabaster slab within these caves, clad head to toe in golden plate-mail armour, brought to him by gods as old as the Kennedy administration, just as—he'll have you know—a famous bard laid a blade upon his shoulder during a party at the condo of a gallery owner somewhere in Manhattan.

For, once he awoke, pushed the stone from the entrance, and emerged into the dazzling light of this new world, saw the multitude of kittens caught in trees, the hags without the strength to carry groceries, the scabrous orcs gnawing bones upon the stinking heath, he wondered, was not what he had done for seven centuries a better way to spend his time? Of course, it wasn't so.

Even now he can hear the voices singing. Even now the trumpets blare. Even now the spangles of confetti, the streamers from the windows of the towers of Waterdeep, the ribbon like skeins of blood unfurl for the return at last of this true and virtuous lord.

DESCENT INTO AVERNUS

Carried aloft in the hands of Tymora, goddess of luck—who is not without a sense of humour—I return, floating down on silver wings to this burning, stinking hell, this bleeding haemorrhoid, this literal asshole of the world where I grew up, where the bards speak and sing in tones as cutting edge as a rotary phone, a tape deck, a killick, or a sundial, where the lighthouse beam seen from above conjures a muzzle-flare of joy—imagining my father's funeral. How once he levelled his rifle at the face of our neighbour across the road whose chickens our Blue Belton ravaged, having snapped their necks and flung their bloody bodies high into the azure sky above our heads. The man had only dared complain.

A muzzle-flare of joy because he's gone? Or because the throne is free for my ascension? Which already happened, truth be told, just ask any one of my ex-girlfriends. Jaws work their stick of spearmint, the earbuds sunk so deep into my skull Gabor Maté's voice is like the voice of God, if God were kind, while the flight attendant takes my plastic cup, my empty bag of chips. The police arrived, and to a spike stuck in the ground thereafter the hungry dog was chained.

DESERT OF DESOLATION

Under this baking sun we've commandeered an enchanted vessel forged of elven steel as thin as crystal, raised on blades like skates that skim across a desert sea of glass upon whose surface is reflected the devastating brightness of the sky. On deck beneath the tarps erected for our shade, we hear the snapping of the sails, see the far-off pyramid where within its crypt it's said the pharaoh has blinked awake his yellow eyes, flexed the rotten tendons of his jaws, and seeks the resurrection of his wife with magic that will bring about the ruin of our world.

Once, a doctor gave me twenty tabs of Valium for the panic that would rise like a wave of dust within my lungs. Told me I should go for walks, take deep breaths, drink a glass of water, bring an awareness to the edges of my body.

They call it the geographical cure—not my first nor last, nor yours. In a future brought about by our adventure here, your hair is lighter from the sun, sand drying on hands that will turn the key in the ignition of the car that takes you back to Waterdeep, where all our trouble first began.

THE RISE OF TIAMAT

Suddenly overcome from listening to a song I used to play back to back to back to back to back in the first apartment I had long ago in art school that crawled with cockroaches whose twitching antennae put me in mind of the landlord's brows—furrowed and reddened after yet another bounced check—I remember the worried phone call from my mother, who for years lived in the swamp whose fetid banks were strewn with bones and bottles, saying she had seen an image of the dragon god who raised its five great heads from out the murk, from the slit window of the hut she'd made from mud while she fed the birds with pearls of dew from points of straw and magic spells, the words of which she learned before the cataclysm that saw her dad die on the street outside their house in December 1977—his head in snow as red as wine stains on a tablecloth, the blood of Christ cupped in a chalice cut from ice. *A family's like a loaded gun. You point it in the wrong direction, someone's going to get killed.*

RRAKKMA

Beneath the ground, the sons of Gith are warring, one against the other, with magic swords forged in the deep or spells whose words cast their enemies into a sleep from which they wake hungover—if they ever wake at all—within the walls of the county jail.

How can it be that the one who says he fucked his brother's wife and beat his brother half to death with a copper pipe ripped from the plumbing underneath the kitchen sink—who remembered not a thing until he stood before the judge—can here weep disconsolate beside the KFC in the food court of the shopping mall because his calico escaped and now it's late November? He who wants to know how there can be a God or peace or solitude in such a world as this, where the most meek and gentle creatures are subject to the most casual and catastrophic whims.

THE RUINS OF UNDERMOUNTAIN

for Gregory Bennett

Of course, of course, the famous lightfoot halfling with his trademark lyre, who seems to like to dress like Ringo Starr off Sgt. Pepper's, is crowned the Bard of Waterdeep. His father was the Open Lord for forty years, which no one seems to mention, but we know how these things go. Plus, the songs he sings, the funny tales he tells, were stolen from some folk I know who broke their bones down in the forge or died with a hammer in their hands. What do we say to those outside the city walls without a nib for bread or mead, when they hear the riotous applause from the highest windows of the castle's tower?

We'd see him here in the Field Ward beyond the gates where the refugees from all the wars—class and otherwise—had settled because they couldn't pay the city's taxes and had nowhere else to go. We'd see him—so artfully dishevelled, caked in drying mud, the studded leather armour that had never tasted steel—and we'd roll our eyes so hard as to sound the clapper in the bell the watchmen ring when they spot a horde of orcs on the horizon. But the orcs have never bothered us—they only ever need a place to stay, and are, in fact, more like us than those behind the merlons and the crenels.

Drunk and picking fights, begging for a blackened eye to show soft-handed princes back at Court, the ladies for whom that title is still a compliment. He even went so far as to live here for a while, for no other reason than to say he had. To those of us whose most practised expertise lay in heavy drinking, it was a joke. But then again, like all of us, I'm sure he has his troubles, the least of which is that he's three feet tall.

THE KEEP ON THE BORDERLANDS

Out here we live in squalor, eating dirt and dandelion leaves boiled in bitter water bubbling green, where rising steam makes us into ghosts. My mother dons a cloak, becomes the walls, a rag-bag lichen texture flocked in faux-velvet burgundy inspired by the Victorian Age—like everything about us, in poor taste.

To live we gorge like animals on poisoned fruit black with mould at its festered heart, yet to us its sweetness spins the magic of the heavens. Its taste is smoke, likewise our lives, that swirls from fires men had set out at the edge to keep the bugbears from our doors, and failed—my mouth a silent x.

It's gotten so I cannot tell what is real from what is not. On holy days, the courtiers come in carriages drawn by horses whose hides are brushed to such a sheen as to match the gleam of the silver bars of the Capital's menagerie.

TALES FROM THE YAWNING PORTAL

Beside the hospital where I was born—its white brick ruins now scattered dragon bones where twisted rusting iron rods jut up, cinder blocks inscribe a chalky spine into the grass, the holes of which are choked with leaves of winter-cress and marrow—my mom house-sits for halflings prone to histrionics. She met them both in Al-Anon. They winter in Bordeaux. She left the happy tenement where first I learned what my hands are for—to roll a twenty-sided die, to hold a pen, a sword, to paw the clicker back and forth between streams of scrambled porn.

GHOSTS OF SALTMARSH

So, is this the road we trudge to happy destiny? The shit-fuelled bog beside emits a light that comes apart and clusters now and then nearby in wisps that lead to nowhere in particular, that refer to nothing other than themselves. The trees whose roots are likewise fed with shit yet thrive, or at least survive—the water red with rusted metal parts and junk, in the shifting shade and light.

I took my daughter to the trail where the riverbanks are kissed with white bellies of the poisoned trout, the sheen of others' scaly sides yet darting in the current's pull. The glimmered rocks change shape before us. Should it get easier? Each time the wizard casts their spell?

LIMBO

DIVINE CONTENTION

For help I'm told I need to find a higher power but for thirty years the solitary Power that I found was me—which wasn't much—whose only lifted finger was the middle. Thought very little of myself yet thought of very little else.

When things got worse, the nurse congratulated me on finding alcohol because along with coke and sex it is the magic that animates the dead. At least you're still alive, she said.

When you cried out to God, was it He who answered and brought you comfort? Fed you and played the lyre? Cast dancing lights so you could see the will-o-wisps and built a fire in the shadow of the mountain where the dragon slept? Was it He? Was it He who led you through the ruins?

DWELLERS OF THE FORBIDDEN CITY

After we were hunted through a jungle overrun with grungs, whose skin secretes a psychedelic poison thick as aloe sap, and discovered the ruins of a city flattened by some ancient angry god when his consort chose mortality in the pursuit of human love, I see you've texted me—after seven months of silence—*Hi I miss you sorry* with a bloody cartoon heart.

The granite columns thick with creepers, black with scorch, the temple crumbling on its hill. On a dais in the centre of what was once this city, our paladin died from wounds he'd taken weeks before—we'd watched him wither with his fever, felt his ghost ascend into the sky as a wisp of smoke. No gold or time—nor even the desire—for a resurrection, we left his body on the brick and pushed into the jungle canopy so dark your hand before your very eyes simply isn't there.

LOCATHAH RISING

How far, and for how long, can this peaceful race of intelligent fish be pushed unto the very brink, before their king instills within their ranks, which are legion, instills within their multitudes of unhatched eggs, the mindless lust for conquest?

Does she know, this hapless, doe-eyed Chapters clerk—sixteen years old at most with a mind composed of Cardi B and cotton candy—the crime against humanity that is her kingdom's unfaced book of lore? That the sight of its spine crammed into the stacks, as fleeting as the shimmer of a betta in the empty eye of a ceramic skull, behind the crenels of its tiny castle, is in itself an act of war? If she does not, it is his grim and happy work to teach her.

As for me, the fetid water at the banks beside the path, strewn with bones and broken glass, bottle caps and vape pods, cigarette ends and discarded rubbers, is not a mirror but a door through which—if I can keep my big trap shut—some angel yet may see and sing and step into the light.

THE DRAGON OF ICESPIRE PEAK

Are they aware, these Fellow Travellers, these grotesques, of how the orcs were made from elves? How the blood that forms the bruise that forms the map that led the party here was inscribed upon the skin of those they claim to love and sought, as in the way that God is sought, to murder?

How the music of the morning that saw me crawl down to the church was not the ringing of the bells, nor the gulls, the docks, nor the noonday gun that's fired for the benefit of tourists off the cruise ship in the harbour, but the clatter of overturned furniture, the crash and bang of a box spring thrown down a narrow stairwell? Do they know the things I can't or won't describe? Do they know, even as they bring me in and welcome me, the perfect magic that these hands so recently had wrought?

RIME OF THE FROSTMAIDEN

Here beneath the glacial ice, where in a previous age a floating city fell and was entombed, where its spires are perfect gleaming through the walls of glass, where my granddad ossified himself with his own cologne, mouthwash, solvent, or whatever he could find, and spent his days with a paper bag to huff, and begged for change, and kept nearby a room to recover from his blackouts, we have brought our party and set ourselves to lay to rest his wife, a bony wraith who haunts these lands with hands drained of their blood.

The parents in the nearby village hold their children tight, for in the endless wintery nights there comes her howling song, the stink of menthol cigarettes she smoked, one lit from the red tip of another.

What difference does it make, should our resolve remain a day, a year, or several? We scale the glacier's mount with rope and spikes stuck in its face and climb so high as to see the curvature of the world, how the solar winds burn the sky with light.

RAVENLOFT

Here a hamlet grown of bitter apples. Beset by mist and vampire spawn—the belfry thick with bats and campy accents, while far above a goth lord weeps into a goblet brimmed with blood. In Berlin I took a box of wine—supremely cheap—to the outdoor rink, strapped on skates and guzzled, wiped my chin and wept, wobbled, wasted, bashed my face into the ice to the merriment of locals. *I'm a writer!* I shouted at their smirking backs.

In Alexanderplatz a gothic horror castle emerges from the rocky crags, sluiced with rain that drives like stakes into the mud beside the TV tower. I crawled into its dusky church and prayed to any god that listened.

As a boy my teeth were rotten agate shards. They pulled them out with rubber-handled vice grips, or so I dreamt—the mask the nurse in spooky whites put on my face was like a hand that smelled of cotton candy. I felt the warmth throb down my body and heard a magic word, *desflurane,* that set me on this path through mountain peaks alit with lightning, post-traumatic stress disorder—she waved bye-bye as I went under.

HUNT FOR THE THESSALHYDRA

In this 1980s nostalgia nightmare, set to synth, ambient and ominous, to strip-mall glass and neon, everyone is goth, or punk, no or new wave, or is a nerd, has never heard of Ronald Reagan, the Contra War, Co Intel Pro. And like everybody else, the hydra only seeks to monetize its trauma, desires only gold and blood, a niche fanbase with the dedication of a cult. Forced to live within these caves beneath the ground where we've been sent to cut its heads off, to bring them back to show the king the game has reached its end—for now, depending on the press, on sales, at which time some evil and enterprising priest will raise it from the dead.

In all these forty years, since before it even had the language for it, the beast has dreamt of nothing other than drugs and drinking, risky sex, freedom from the tyranny of work, and death to its enemies, who are multitude and ready, practised and precise in the service of their lords.

OUT OF THE ABYSS

At that time the layers of the Abyss were equal to the number of the Beast, but Wizards of the Coast later changed it to infinity. Quaint to think that devil worship was thought to be a risk for kids when in this house threats of murder-suicide were as commonplace as frozen fries, as hot dogs boiling on the stove.

From our '82 Chevette I took the tire jack, hitched my sweater on the barbwire fence that ringed the junkyard, beat the headlights from as many wrecks as times "Abracadabra" played on the radio—which was a lot—and through some rageful transmutation opened up a door into the Underdark, where a life of petty crime lay before me. I heard the metal sing for the kingdom that had come.

The kingdom that had come. Demogorgon, this behemoth Prince of Demons, turned his two great gibbon heads. Turned his two great snapping jaws. Turned his red and burning eyes. Turned the suckered tentacles for arms. Turned the scaly toes toward the surface of the world.

THE HIDDEN SHRINE OF TAMOACHAN

Here where the makers of this module have appropriated a culture other than their own for profit, I find myself beneath some Aztec pyramid that doubles as my dank, dump apartment—post-divorce. Ten years of wedded bliss for this—a cardboard box full of leaves from my last abandoned novel, whose status as *abandoned* remains my one and only wise artistic choice. My cupboards bare but for a can of lighter fluid, but why should I add arson to the list of sordid crimes my ex has publicized in the local press? Did I or did I not fuck a twentysomething swimsuit-model waitress?

The unicorn whose desiccated head we'd cut off and kept at the bottom of the deep freeze, where ice cubes cloaked in fuzzy snow were the only thing to eat. Had it known the beauty of its horn? A spiralled conch like some iridescent dildo I wish my wife had brought up to her lips to blow a warning call to the dumb degenerate to come: this older, haunted version of myself, more skeletal, more pale, led by his master through the raucous, jeering crowds for no other purpose than to show his grinning skull to all.

And now and now and now they say to wait for the miracle to happen, but will the miracle pay for my litigation? My heat and light? My food? Above the ground, among the market square's sweltered throngs, the cultists sing and come for me, the cultists sing and come for me, the cultists sing for the second coming of their god, whose most pious first demand is abstinence, or death.

DUNGEON OF THE MAD MAGE

Glimpsed from a sloop hewn from the husks of giant mushroom stalks where the grey dwarves and fish-folk mine and ply these humid caves, in the muck the miracle of a common grackle whose blue head a bulb of neon, whose iridescent body up to now I'd never known to pray for someone else to see.

As for myself it was the junkyard, Waterdeep, and the bonfires of Dragondown—its effigies stuffed with cloth and straw and kindling, the falling gleam on branches and the crabgrass of a river that had swamped its banks, whose rusty grate was clogged with trash and brambles, and freezing rain and fog so cold there were particles of ice held in its breath, plaques on stumps along the trail to commemorate cats and dogs that died, the cedar waxwings drunk on berries raving in the trees, the terror that morning by the docks when you held me, gave me your last tab of Valium against your better judgement, all this shit I've put you through, I suppose when this is done I shall to you as well have to pay amends, but also say thank you—thank you for staying here with me, my friend.

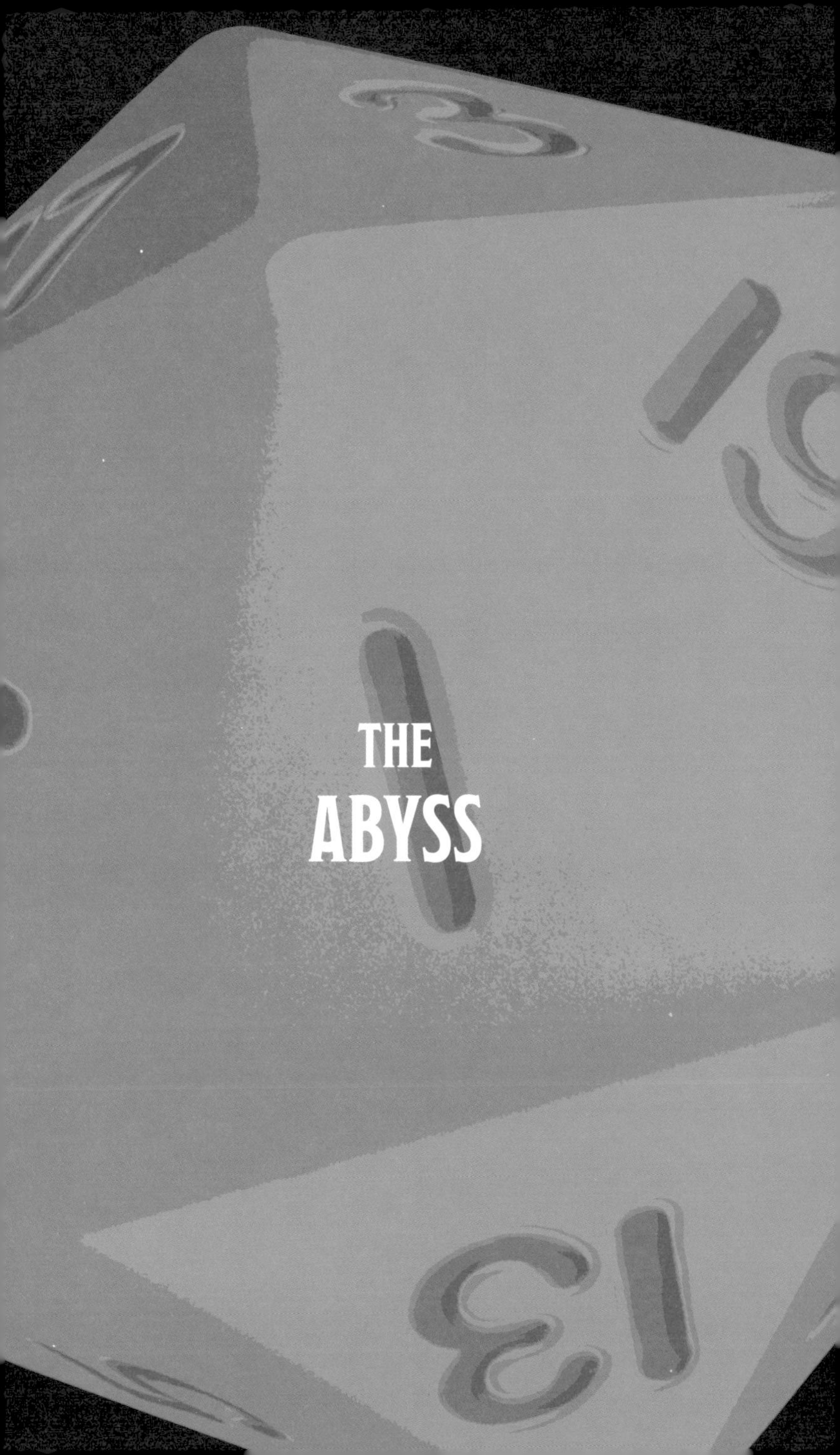

THE ABYSS

THE FORGOTTEN TEMPLE OF THARIZDUN

Like Keats, that most cucked of romantics, choking to death in Rome, the cure I sought I thought lay in Beijing, beside the church a billionaire had built to honour gods of Contemporary Art, wherein I'd lately tacked my own feeble offering to the cause, drinking *baiju* in the alley with a crowd of locals who I dream work in some nearby factory, plotting a wildcat strike, a true and widespread end to hierarchy.

At night the streets are thronged outside a retro discotheque where I've befriended two wacko drugged-up Czechs insistent on a threesome, and my burning eyes are fingers up the legs of walnut trees on the meridian, where ten lanes of zipping traffic fume the air with violet.

Is this the gold that you were seeking? With your drudgery and toil? This carousel of moderate success? Back home your cokehead wife is sleeping with the inbred second son of a royal house that teeters on the very brink of farce. And you can think of nothing in this state but the burnished doors of the temple where you saw her last, as she was wrenched soundless from her saddle in the jaws of the dragon that swooped from out the blazing sun.

STORM LORD'S WRATH

On Icespire Peak where the high road cuts through foothills to the Sword Mountains that arc like a boomerang beside the detox clinic, to which I've returned more times than there are fermented berries in the April trees, past a brackish mere that's ringed in knotweed and spiny cattails bending, amid the crags a town abandoned, and in the town her empty tower crept with ivy.

After the rain that fell the night a storm swept in above the peaks and stung our heads with sound and hail, and we beheld the face of God formed in its thunderhead, I put my hand between her thighs which yawned and formed a goblet's mouth—felt her hip bone jut and thrust while she was holding up her skirt. My sponsor says he isn't sure that sex is not my drug of choice.

Should she step out and lean against the rail and see me on the ground where I'm incapable of getting up without a gulp of crisp Chablis that dews the bottle's lip with jewels as glossy as the spider-webs that span the branches of the mountain ash. Should she step out of an archway like a myth and lean against the rail and see.

DRAGON HEIST

For seven weeks post-probation I had a squalid top-floor dive on Fish Street in the Dock Ward of Waterdeep, crown jewel of the North, the only redeeming quality of which was a holly bush in the alleyway whose leaves were hard and sharp enough to cut my coke into a portrait of my father's face. I was supremely confident and afraid I was bipolar—eked out a modest life on garnets, amber, whatever golden dragons I could rob or borrow from those whom I was sure I'd never see again, including him.

Then I had my daughter and nothing changed inside of me like I'd been told it would. I drank and used for two years after that before I gave it up for good, I hope—her last birthday I was present.

Griffin-riding watchmen crossed the sky in silver armour shining like the city lights, but they would never know the beauty of my work—in that room I scratched the magic words into my book, wrote the spells that brought the gold and jewels and blood into the light, conjured and became the god I had invented.

WHITE PLUME MOUNTAIN

Because of who my father was, or his father, or the father before him, or many others, stretching back perhaps to the time before this world was formed, grew ripe, grew rotten, when the gods made war against their brethren—I was forced to leave this town with a dagger and my wits, provisions very nearly indiscernible from nothing. Stole a camper-van the floor and walls of which were black with soot, the single bed a slab of fetid foam, a diesel engine that ground itself into a fist of molten iron at the fork leading north or east. On foot I left the stinking husk behind, saw the spires of the mountains shimmer in the far-off fading dim and cursed myself for having blood that flowed, that was the same as his.

Near here a half-elf farmer gave me food for work, a pen inside the stable where I slept. I combed the olives from the slender branches in the fields and watched them fall into a net of nylon neon-green like the lights that wrote the name above the door of the only dive where I still happened to be welcome. Sometimes at night the smell and taste of straw and shit, the night air crisp as vodka iced in a flask of crystal like the ship I dream will take me back to that I have so loved and lost forever.

TOMB OF HORRORS

To the cloistered Incel devotees among whom I am strangely, happily numbered, the adventure that we're on has been termed a thresher, and it is, it is, for here I am, amongst this party of middle-aged men, these titans of countless wars, these veterans of office gossip and junior management, each one a nightmare beneath our clothes, each one either in, or avoiding, yoga class and therapy.

What would drive a wizard, undead or otherwise, to wreak such wanton destruction on those he claimed to love? And then to hide himself beneath the ground, within this tomb, designed with so many deadly traps and tricks as to remain alone forever. Two hundred spikes at the bottom of a pit, a silver mist that drops your intelligence score to one. His spell-book a list of crimes, a list of names of those to whom he has promised to one day make amends, should he ever rise again, which isn't likely, and in truth, who would ever want to see him coming? The bony hands held out in supplication, for the thousandth time.

THE CITY OF SKULLS

I took this path against my will—beside the river banked in Queen Anne's Lace white as bones beneath the soil through which they grow and seethe and sway—because the means of my survival, as my sponsor says, once again had turned against me.

The shit that's on my mind—what difference does it make? The hand that rolls the dice or ties the knot or pulls the blade or twists the cap or sets the hammer in its notch is the same that strokes my daughter's cheek, brings a mouth as cold as iron to my lips to drink.

EXPEDITION TO THE BARRIER PEAKS

In all their furious splendour, the gods at last came down on me. Cold I woke beside the sea where I heard the forklifts loading crates, the hammers of the blacksmiths in the forge.

At the church the priest gave me his horse, the saddlebags stuffed with strips of jerk, hardtack, dried fruit, and nuts—I tipped the waterskin and felt its silver in my throat. Near the peaks where the townsfolk say a wraith has plans for each and every one of us, I saw the bodies of the Grand Duke's men, splayed within the thorny brush, picked at by the crows. Their beaks bright in the sun recall last night: the glare my iPhone's flashlight cast as I crawled through broken glass and trash outside my place where I had somewhere lost my keys.

THE SINISTER SECRET OF SALTMARSH

The cliffs beside the town are plum with phlox and foxglove where you said you'd drive the car into the sea three hundred feet below. My baby brother crying in the back. A cave far down the face where jagged rocks are lashed with waves. Upon a ridge mossed with kelp, the skeletons of sculpin, the merfolk sun their iridescent scales and watch the swell for that which stalks them from beneath. Wind whistling through aeolian caves whose mouths were eaten there by salt, the tide that drops a malleus down upon an anvil. I hear your voice like water trapped, thrumming in my ear.

The ocean fed a saltwater marsh, beside which lay our home—the wrecks of junkyard cars, their twisted, gleaming hulls. Last night I heard the sea-hag wailing from beneath the bog, her child somewhere inside those sunken husks.

My mother calls. I tell her that I'm fine.

THE GATES OF FIRESTORM PEAK

When the town drunk went missing, against the protestations of the townsfolk, and indeed against our own better judgement, we tracked him up this mountain path through bitten stunted trees turned black with soot that spumes from the molten peak of blood and ash that looms above this valley.

Once an age, once in a millennium, when at night a certain star streaks the sky above our village, within the peaks there swings ajar the crystal gate that bars that world from this. They say that he went mad, or madder than he was, but we didn't know the man. Didn't know that to cross its threshold meant there was no going back. And even had we known, who between us would have chosen differently?

My kid brother now grown and a bloody-minded ranger for whom still I feel a terrible responsibility. Bound together by a magic deeper and more hateful even than the peaks are high and cold. We snapped branches off the nearby trees, made beds of bows beneath a fallen fir and sat down to watch the dark, the gaps between the needles where we could see the sky, the far-up mountaintop upon which countless of our kin have died between the jaws of what remains incomprehensible to us—he sleeps with hands clutched to his heart, his face beside the fire an orange moon of light.

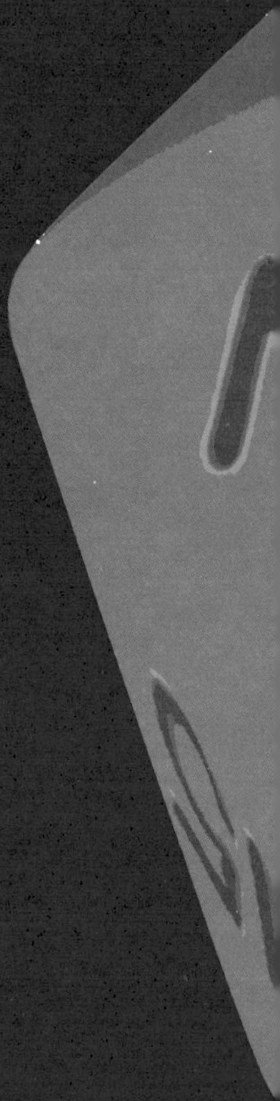

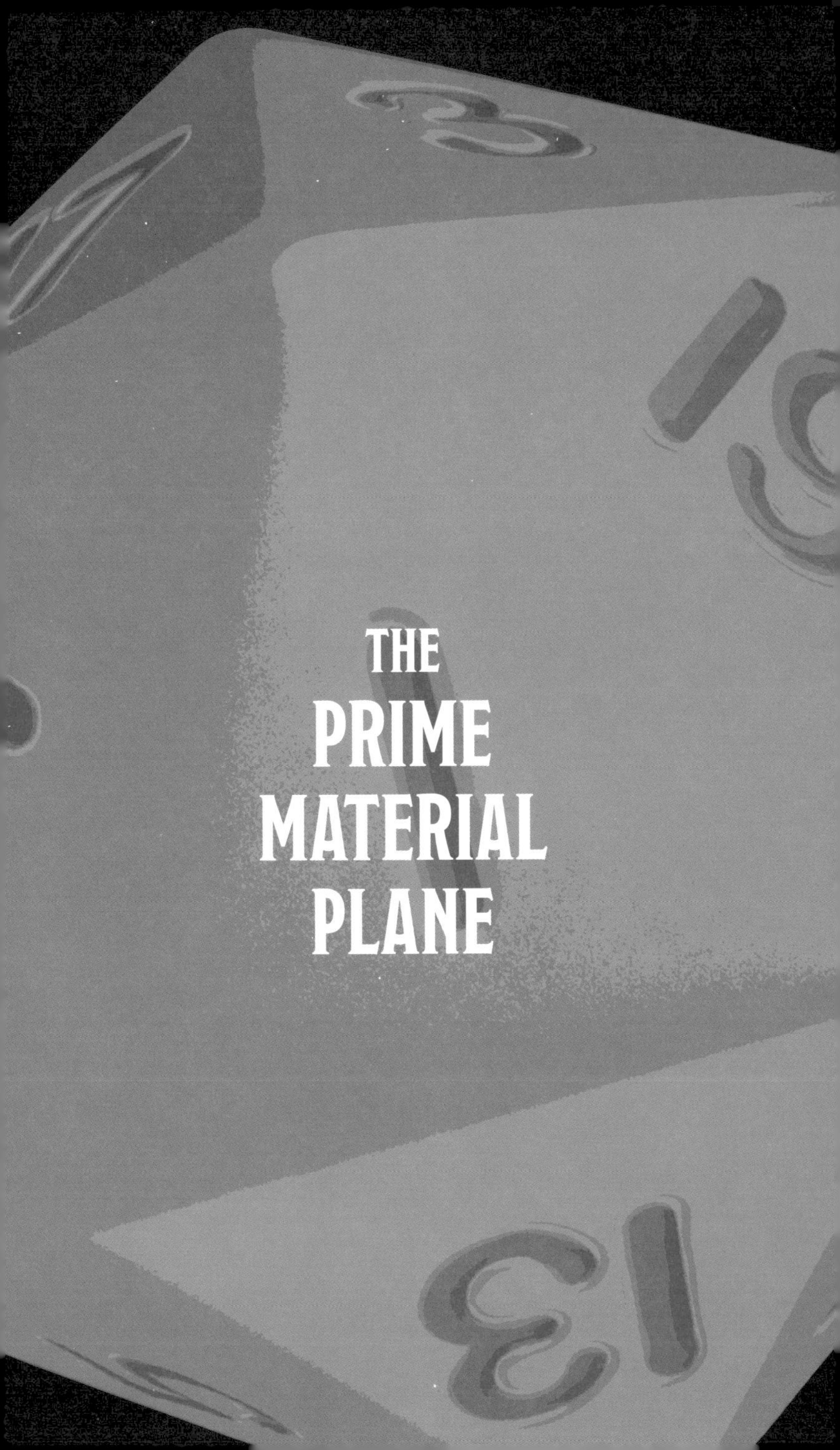

THE PRIME MATERIAL PLANE

THE ISLE OF DREAD

for the residents of the island of Newfoundland

So far removed from those kingdoms that I knew, and loved, I can hardly remember them. The valleys green as stems from seeds through which my most troubling entanglements have flourished. The verdant country where a century before the veins of the Republicans in Spain were opened up like mouths by bayonets, where in the purple shade of the Pyrenees I fell in love with Anarchism, and out of love with the yuan-ti travelling companion whom I said I'd one day marry. I took this blasted rock beset by vicious tides to hide and lick my wounds.

For here this dive is swarmed with creatures freshly crawled out of the muck—all of whom I'd like to fuck, or at the very least, to tolerate. In the bathroom mirror at the sink, smudged with red and glitter-dust, the arrows of the orcs agleam with drugs point up to gods who shrug and giggle, bored to tears that bleed into my beer. I smash a bottle over someone's head—who cares? Run out the door and home to where I still wait for the City Watch to knock, prepared to blame an evil twin.

They say beneath this wasteland's tephra spine a womb of ancient rock is ripe with amber fruit. A pinch of flash-powder sets an instant onto paper. I sit at this machine, the magic box, the tool of transmutation. I'm told she later left for Montreal, wed an architect and had two sons, the first of which was born without a trachea.

RETURN TO THE TOMB OF HORRORS

Up this crumbling tower whose spiral stairs are carpeted in cowslip and creeping moonflower—shackled by a band of pig-headed orcs whose malice I mistook for mercy—I'm dragged to the door of my mom's apartment where I've been living with my daughter since the breakup, trying to ignore the obvious. The law requires them to see me safe inside, must verify I am the one I say I am, for I've lost my wallet somewhere in the graveyard where they tracked me down running through the dark and plucked me from the sodden ground where I had tripped and fallen.

I rap my bloody knuckles on her door, which opens. There comes a pause before she can admit this creature is her son. Six months before right there on the linoleum where now my blood drips out a Morse code, I found our cat whose corpse was stiff as shit with rigor mortis—heard its thud like a bass drum kick when I threw it in the dumpster down below the window where I saw the shadows of the hippogriffs gun and whirl across the lot as quick as buckshot. It isn't true that the agents of the king hold a monopoly of violence, for there are many of his subjects pleased to help them with their work.

PRINCES OF THE APOCALYPSE

The flames and the flames and the flames and the flames and the billowing flames and the world's greatest role-playing game and who am I to judge a grown man for pretending to be someone other than himself, when the self in question is a monster and a loser? Which is not hyperbole, depending on who you ask, particularly if the one you ask is him, despite the fact that there can be no monsters and no losing, just patrimony, and bad luck, a horrible demise, and the flames.

On the trade route north, beside the Sumber Hills, where a thousand years ago the dwarves drove out the hordes and erected keeps to guard against them, I've travelled to fix my parents' marriage through some fabled retroactive magic. It will never work, and my friends—the hero and the clown and the lost child derived from self-help literature—are oblivious to the time my ex was forced to call the cops because her boyfriend was again someone other than himself, or maybe just himself, and had gripped her arm in such a vise as to bruise an arcane map of purple ink. An arcane map of purple ink that led the party here.

CURSE OF STRAHD

How lonely must it be to live forever, abstinent of sun or running water, of gods or mirrors, without a shadow, waiting for an invite that will never come? He who stalks his limestone parapet high above us all, casting spells on whatever farmer's daughter strikes his fancy, has cranked The Cure so loud the windows in the village rattle, cracking in their frames.

A sea of peaks like broken teeth above this sleeping town the fields of which are blessed with dreaming cows whose eyes are milk-glass marbles underneath their lids—stock-still in mounds of clover licked with glassy frost that glimmers like the vials of holy water the townsfolk keep beside their beds. The bats and rats and wolves are said to be his servants, singing "Friday I'm In Love."

We lived beside the Brandenburg bridge where such acts of saccharine puppy love as a dime-store lock inscribed with our initials snapped upon its iron rail was as much as we had wits to muster. Why should this put one in mind of a heart or fist caught in a throat, a polyp in a windpipe? I was incapable of speech, of anything, about to be a father—watched the sun descend beyond the concrete coffin slabs of the Holocaust Memorial.

FROZEN SICK

One thousand years, or a hundred, or merely forty-four, or a single day—it's all the same, they say, which isn't true, but it helps the newly sober gird their loins for what's to come, or isn't, depending only on the bones, whatever god you can imagine.

Was it because he chose the honey cruller, and not the Boston cream? Dried his hands with toilet paper because there wasn't any paper towel? Was it because our table had been taken by a crew of latte bikers on our Sunday afternoon, and so from where he sat he couldn't see the window? Its plate glass, its light, and how the light was falling.

THE ASSASSIN'S KNOT

He used a length of nylon cord no longer than a man is tall—a neon yellow brighter than the gleam along the edge of a blade that strings the throats of orcs with red, the line the sunrise made out in the wilderness near Salmonier where he fished trout and salmon shooting quick as arrows up the white foam of the falls—and looped it through the hole the electrician bored into the basement joist from which the dusty snarls of knob-and-tube were pulled, stuck there since the house was built back when his dad came home from the Western Front, grinning and insane from the monstrosities he'd seen and heard and done and likewise then became—an acolyte of some squid-headed god whose beak would snap the bones of the virtuous and villainous alike—the glowing skin of new wiring throughout the horse-hair walls.

RETURN TO THE TEMPLE OF ELEMENTAL EVIL

Why should it be that the mounted heads, the VLTs, the red and yellow blinking lights of the retro jukebox in the corner sets the scene for my return, on yet another slip into oblivion, here in the common room of the worst hotel in town, and not some glitzy awards reception for the gift from God that is my poetry?

Is it the drug-dealing and gambling, the prostitution and extortion, the constant threat and actuality of violence overseen by this clutch of elven gangsters—each a sad facsimile of Eminem—that recalls the pleasant seaside brightly painted wagon of my Coney Island fortune-teller? Years ago, before I knew what trouble was. Or is it merely the existence in itself of this tawdry psychodrama?

One eye concealed behind an eyepatch, she crammed my cash into a crimson bra-strap while in her crystal ball a soap opera was playing: Marlena, possessed again by Satan, cheating on her husband. Under such a spell as this, tell me who could fault her for her infidelity?

Like sands through the hourglass, so were the sands beside the boardwalk where I saw a man, who'd struck by chance his hook into the eye of an enormous gannet, unwind the fishing line around its sinewed neck and fling the body back into the sea—laughing as he watched it tumble in the snarling tide.

QUEEN OF THE SPIDERS

Whose bright idea is it to say that every rose has its thorn? That every night has its dawn? Sadly true to my alignment, when the happy news is carried luminescent as a spider egg in the mouth of my ex-girlfriend, I long for nothing other than the forge of Gracklstugh, its furnaces and flues. Its clang and boom, its ceaseless chimneys coughing smoke alit with sparks within a lung of shale. The soot as thick as plumes of spores exhaled from the giant mushrooms that cluster all throughout the caves.

How can it be that the glint of blackened steel, the glimmered orange light within the depths, makes one such as myself yearn for the deeper darkness that I knew, down beneath the surface of the world, in a back-alley bar with a desire that burned for an everlasting blackout?

That clang and boom, that womb, that tomb, that blessed room in which I drank, resenting her bedazzled denim, her cowboy boots, her dumb tattoos, her big fake boobs, her taste in music I had failed so utterly to mould. How could anyone in their right mind love Poison, and how could anyone in their right mind love anyone who does?

STORM KING'S THUNDER

Was it the Elvis Presley? The cars on blocks? The salmon fishing? The bottom drinking, the bike stealing, the junkyard, or the pornography? Or rather was it on these rags and skins, this straw and kindling, where the thorn and bramble forms of effigies were set for burning to commemorate the past and to ward against its coming back, that I cut my teeth? That I first reached up and held the hand of Gruumsh, the One-Eyed God of Orcs? How haunted must he have been to do such things as playing dead—then to laugh because I was weak enough to need him? Was it derision, on his part? Or relief that indeed I did?

Was it he, or someone else, whose essence matched the smoke that rose once the bonfires were lit and stoked with lengths of snotty var and tamarack stolen by the city watch, when they dispersed and pacified the shantytowns outside the parapet to the cheers of those within, including him and I?

For even then I knew there were worse things in this world than ancient wyrms, or cultists clutching swords and daggers forged from dragon teeth, or arctic trolls who grow back limbs as quick and silver as a rabbit foot, a spell component plucked in desperation from a belt pouch, a talon pushed into the chamber of a gun.

HOARD OF THE DRAGON QUEEN

So this, this, this is the miracle that happens? Saturday night, and how did this former walking fireball—a total babe by all accounts (especially my own)—get so old and dumb and ugly? Painting pewter miniatures in a floral apron of my mother's, an LED light on a headband magnifier, half watching the hockey game with a can of Diet Sprite.

Tiamat, my true and only love, whose beauty I first beheld when I was thirteen and had my first encounter with the cops. Tiamat, in whose thrall there is nothing but the next catastrophic thrill. Tiamat, my five-headed dragon god with wings as wide as all the realms, wonders what I'll do when my unemployment finally runs out, when my daughter hits puberty, when mom dies and I'll have no one left to talk to. Her breath is elemental. Her breath could burn the flesh right off your bones and burn the bones to ash. O Tiamat, what made you the monster that you are? She sweeps her shadow swift as rain against my bedroom window as she soars into the night. There's a party somewhere, and everyone is there.

LOST LABORATORY OF KWALISH

The long crawl out from the cave like a lung that lives beneath this mountain this passage like an oesophagus this passage up into this meeting room its cracked linoleum its instant coffee its burning dust on baseboard heaters. My sponsor says there are rooms like this in every town and city in the world like a network of the radically serene which isn't true but it makes a pretty picture.

Into this mouth the long passage. Into this mouth where words incantations and the way in which we're traumatized makes a perfect match, is the hammer in its notch. Hell my friends hello my friends we made it to this day which is today hello.

ACKNOWLEDGEMENTS

The italicized lines at the end of "The Rise of Tiamat" on page 20 are drawn from Belle and Sebastian's song "I Could Be Dreaming."

An earlier sequence from this collection won *subTerrain*'s Lush Triumphant Award for Poetry and was published therein in 2023. Several other of these poems subsequently appeared in *Riddle Fence*.

Financial support from the City of St. John's, ArtsNL, and the Canada Council for the Arts was crucial during the writing and editing of these poems.

Thanks to Rebecca Rose and the team at Breakwater Books for believing in this collection, and to Mark Callanan for his thoughtful editorial support throughout.

Deepest gratitude to Neria Aylward, Audrey Rees-Power, and to the L.A.W. of Candlekeep.

CRAIG FRANCIS POWER (he/him) is a St. John's-based multidisciplinary visual artist and the award-winning author of three novels: *Blood Relatives*, *The Hope*, and *Skeet Love*. *Total Party Kill* is his first collection of poetry.